The backbone of Bangladesh's development

Bangladesh's development : The challenges and ways of addressing

Md Bayazid Khan

ISBN 978-93-5610-243-9
© Md Bayazid Khan 2022
Published in India 2022 by Pencil

Contributors:
Editor: Mst. Nahid Parvin
Editor: Mst. Nahid Parvin

A brand of
One Point Six Technologies Pvt. Ltd.
123, Building J2, Shram Seva Premises,
Wadala Truck Terminal, Wadala (E)
Mumbai 400037, Maharashtra, INDIA
E connect@thepencilapp.com
W www.thepencilapp.com

Author biography

Author of the book, Md Bayazid Khan was born in Bangladesh. He is a master degree holder in Economics. He has been working in the primary education sector in Bangladesh since 1997. He has experience of working as Upazila Education Officer, Assistant District Primary Education Officer and District Primary Education Officer. He visited the United Kingdom and Malaysia to receive training on primary education management, school management, facilitation of training, material development etc. His wife also has been working for the primary education sector since 1996 and has experience of working as Assistant Upazila Education Officer & Upazila Education Officer. His father, Md Harunur Rashid Khan was a service holder who died in 2017 and his mother, Payara Begum is a housewife. They have a son, Mohammad Areeb Sharar of sixteen years old. The author has been writing articles for the renowned national English dailies on education and development issues of Bangladesh since 2012. His two books, 'Enlightening People for a Developed Bangladesh' and 'Road to build tomorrow's Bangladesh' were published in 2016 & 2020 respectively.

CONTENTS

The backbone of Bangladesh's development

Traditionally, the people of Bangladesh and the government are emotional and visionary. Before going to sleep at night, each and every citizen of the country expects a better tomorrow. The visionary government is also committed to build a developed Bangladesh by 2041 where citizens will be able to live peaceful, prosperous and happy lives like a developed country's citizens. People become optimistic as the country has achieved status of a middle-income country in 2021. The process of development is now visible to the citizens as they are witnessing ongoing development works of mega projects like the Padma Bridge, Matarbari & Ruppur Electricity Plant, Metro Rail, introduction of Export Processing Zones and IT & High-Tech Parks for encouraging domestic and foreign investors to invest etc all over the country. Development of a country never takes place overnight. It is a continuous process and development of a country can never occur without accelerating growth in all sectors of the economy. It is the outcome of a blend of development-friendly policies in all sectors of the economy and smooth implementation of policies by corruption-free government administrative machinery.

In spite of witnessing government's heartfelt efforts, enormous investment in multifarious development friendly projects and taken initiatives, people become disheartened regarding fulfillment of government' vision of making the country a developed one seeing some irregularities committed by both policy makers and policy implementers. They expect corruption free services from service givers, bureaucratic hazard free responses from public and private offices, availability of pure contamination free food & essential commodities, removal of all sorts of dishonesty, safe movement and co-existence of men and women outside home, available transport facilities without traffic jam and last but not the least performing responsibilities of good citizenship by each and every individual in and outside home. Their aspirations are very much similar to the facilities that the people consume in the developed countries.

The dream of the people of Bangladesh seems to be utopian as there are so many hindrances like a large number of populations, small size of the country, limited natural resources etc. But these can never be the impediments to the process of development in Bangladesh alongside with achieving its peoples' aspiration to make the country a developed one.

If we look at the economic development of China we can't say that our large population is a problem in the process of our development. The developed countries and other countries that have less population are seriously suffering from scarcity of human resources. They are now encouraging people of other countries to become their immigrants.

Singapore is one of the leading economically developed countries in the world. But the area of Singapore is very small. So, small areas of Bangladesh should not be a hurdle for development.

We have limited natural resources like gas, oil, gold and coal, and therefore our development is happening at a snail's pace. But looking at the countries in the Middle East it can be easily said that availability of affluent natural resources may not be the only way to make a country developed. Moreover, we have most valuable resources like fertile land, surface and non-surface water, suitable weather for cultivation and last but not the least hard working people.

So, a large population, limited natural resources and small areas may not be hurdles for development in Bangladesh. The question is why Bangladesh is not much developed after 42 years of its independence? The answer is – the country failed to utilise its natural and human resources in a planned way as well as absence of good governance in providing services by service providers, lack in applying civic senses & maintaining discipline and inability of bringing desired growth in agriculture & industrial sector due to lacking in chalking out suitable plans. Moreover, our political parties and bureaucratic systems badly fail to bring the people of the country to work with unity and commitment for its development.

But Bangladeshi people are never disheartened. They are a brave nation. They have a reputation of rebuilding the country in a short time immediately after the war in 1971.

They are also surviving successfully with the united efforts during natural calamities that hit almost every year. So, to make government as well as people's vision into reality all the political parties, policy makers, concerned authorities responsible for policies carrying into effect and stakeholders need to sit together to come to a consensus to work with commitment and dedication for the sake of fulfilling peoples' dream into reality.

Development of Bangladesh needs gradually advancement in god-gifted natural & human resource dependent economy (agriculture and industry), developed attitude of citizens for applying civic senses, establishing good governance, equal participation of both men and women in economic activities, stable and harmonize political environment and last but not the least maintaining discipline in every sphere of personal, social and work life.

Privileges in agriculture and planned industrialization

Importance of increasing agro-based production & ensuring agro-based industrialization:

Obviously the agriculture sector provides a lifeline for our national economy. So, economic growth of the country mostly depends on growth in the agriculture sector. Moreover, economic emancipation of almost two-thirds of the people depends on agriculture. We have a large population in the country in comparison to the small size of areas. To produce food grains for its entire people the country needs to increase agricultural production. But unplanned industrialisation and urbanisation on the cultivable land, poor marketing system, improper and inadequate storage facilities for perishable agricultural items like fruits, vegetables etc, absence of agro-based industrialisation and intermediaries pocketing profit are creating hurdles to developing the lifeline of the national economy. On the contrary, farmers are compelled to cultivate tobacco, strawberry, flower etc instead of growing major cereal crops only for earning more. Therefore, the government needs to take necessary steps to motivate the farmers to grow more major cereal crops like rice, wheat, pulses etc as well as oilseeds, vegetables, fishes, poultry, livestocks and fruits. Because, the government needs to ensure food for the entire population from domestic sources as it will be costly for importing food grains from abroad. Moreover, almost 90 per cent people of the country are rice eaters. So, the government should encourage farmers providing logistic and financial support alongside bringing all of the cultivable land under cultivation for increasing production of major cereal crops like rice, wheat and pulses. Besides ensuring this, the government should also take necessary steps for growing other agro based crops like vegetables, oilseeds, fishes, poultry, livestock etc to ensure availability of nutrition supplementary foods taken with rice or wheat.

Increased agro-production demands co-operative farming:

Bangladesh is self-sufficient in food production nowadays and the nation really feels proud of it. This success has become possible due to the government's direct intervention in the agricultural sector. Government has provided substantial support to farmers for increasing production. The government has been providing a huge amount of money as subsidy every year in getting available low cost equipment, fertilizers, irrigation facilities etc by farmers. But, if farmers are deprived of gaining profit in return to investment despite growing enormous production, they must lose interest to continue efforts in paddy or other agriculture products cultivation. On the other hand, farmers' frequent loss due to price falling in agriculture products definitely compels the government to consider its policy of providing subsidies on agro-inputs.

Now, the time has come to identify the loss factors of farmers who hardly earned produced paddy and other agro-products. The major factors responsible for price falling are involvement of middlemen or syndicate in selling paddy/rice or other agro-products, government procurement process, farmers inadequate preservation facility and continuing import of rice or paddy in spite of growing huge paddy in a crop season.

To mitigate the problems that are facing farmers for getting reasonable prices for their cultivated products and to minimize undue intervention of the identified major factors responsible for lower prices of agro-products, following ideas have to be taken considered in agriculture sector:

Selling procedures of hardly earned products must be freed from cruel intervention of middlemen or intermediaries. Moreover, the syndicate's intervention to control the market must be stopped. It is also revealed that about 90% farmers depended on the middlemen for marketing of their products and they did not get fair prices from the middlemen because middlemen are playing a marketing role.

Policy regards to import rice/paddy and other agro-products should depend on local growing production.

The Procurement process with a rational fair price considering market rate in harvesting season must be started a bit early so that farmers have the intention of selling products to the government without any hesitation.

There should be adequate preservation facilities with easy access to farmers.

As farmers are losing interest in paddy or other agro-products cultivation due to face loss returns to their investment, so domestic production of agro-products including paddy will decrease alarmingly. In this regard, there could be a crisis in staple food production that will certainly be a threat on food security. In addition, farmers are to face contradictory situations in the form of over production owing to cultivation friendly conducive climate & available facilities and poor production or loss of production due to natural or manmade disasters. Geographically Bangladesh is very ideal for paddy cultivation. Moreover, the fertility of land and climate of the country is so conducive to cultivate and produce satisfactory diversified agro-products beside paddy. Keeping this cultivation friendly atmosphere at the heart of our farming scenario, the country needs to take lucrative measures to keep farmers interested in cultivating. But natural disasters, lack of capital, absence of using improved technology in cultivation, illiteracy in agro-production, complex & time consuming accessibility of government facilities, unavailability of adequate labors, costly participation of moneylenders, small scale farming in the form of fragmented plots of land etc are affecting negatively on agro- production.

In consideration of minimizing adverse effects of aforesaid issues in the agro-sector as well as to remove barriers of getting fair prices of production, farmers and the government may think of introducing a comprehensive scheme of Co-operative Farming. Under co-operative farming, owners of fragmented lands are to be asked to have their holdings joined in a scheme of helpful partnership with a view to merge the small agricultural holdings in larger co-operative units.

Co-operative is a tested strategy for socio-economic development and however, the movement might be expanded to the agriculture sector to repose farmers' faith in cultivating. It also brings food security to the country and ensures equity regards to economic solvency among farmers and landless people. So, farmers, landowners and all concerned with agro-economy may consider the following advantages of co-operative farming just to introduce the scheme in Bangladesh.

Co-operative cultivation certainly increases production because of using improved technology or methods in cultivation and enabling easy access of quality inputs as input suppliers have competitive interests to deal with the cooperatives for supplying agro-machineries & inputs.

Farmers in the cooperatives have the opportunities of gaining and utilizing skills or knowledge for increasing production by receiving training on best pest control, proper uses of fertilizers, improved seedling, faster harvesting method etc on a regular basis.

Incomes of farmers in the cooperatives must increase due

to multifarious positive impacts of the cooperative like increase production, reduce the cost of production, sell produce with rational price as the co-operatives knowing price information of domestic and international market deal with the buyers on behalf of the farmers etc. Co-operatives shield farmers from exploitation of getting fair price of produce from chain shop owners or importers or intermediaries. Co-operatives are able to sell products at the highest possible price or fair price as these have the advantages of bargaining properly with the buyers or middlemen.

The interest of the farmer is usually the main priority of co-operatives. Challenges like timely payment of produce, providing of loans (From compulsory savings of farmers), medical/education facilities to family members etc might be ensured by the co-operatives. In addition, negotiations on receiving frequently changeable prices of produce and bonuses are usually handled by the co-operatives with the interest of the farmers as their main agenda.

Co-operative farming facilitates timely credit from banks or financial institutions with fair interests by proper bargaining that ensures availability of cultivation needed equipment, inputs, irrigation facilities etc. Apart from that, co-operative certainly assure farmers tension free active participation in production.

Co-operative farming may ensure effective uses of fragmented cultivable and fallow lands by bringing these under cultivation of diverse traditional and non-traditional agro-products. Co-operative can also promote crab or other export-oriented products cultivation in the saline-prone areas of the country as a non-traditional agro-product. Co-operatives have the capability of inaugurating climate-smart cultivation all the year round managing seasonal natural barriers. Co-operatives may create opportunities for farmers to produce diverse crops instead of producing only paddy or wheat. Moreover, integrated cultivation or farming like paddy & fish, fish & duck etc might be introduced conveniently through co-operatives.

Proper storage of food grains in case of over production may become possible by co-operatives that certainly protect farmers from confronting loss due to the poor price of produce. Besides, marketing or exporting of produce with a view to make co-operative cultivation more profitable to farmers than individual cultivation becomes so comfortable and convenient by co-operatives.

Co-operatives may encourage farmers to introduce organic cultivation by providing them with training and logistic support. It also removes food adulteration and contamination effectively.

Co-operative farming however, not only brings benefits to enlisted member farmers but also ensures equity and social justice especially to the landless farmers and sharecroppers. Because they have access to equitable participation in producing, earning and receiving benefits/profits in the co-operatives. Women have significant access to work in the co-operatives as there are scopes of varieties of work only for women. Inauguration of co-operatives might also encourage village people not to go to Dhaka or other cities for earning, thus, stemming the influx of domestic migration for livelihood. Last but not the least, farmers' life in Bangladesh is full of risks as the agriculture sector mostly depends on vagaries of nature. Natural calamities cause massive havoc on farmers' hard earned produce almost every year. Most of the individual farmers can't cope with the risks and uncertainty that prevails in the agriculture sector and thus leave the profession due to being ruined economically. So, co-operatives may take the responsibility of supporting farmers economically and mentally and may take initiatives with the support of the government for minimizing risks.

The government may think of introducing co-operative farming by motivating farmers, landowners and other concerned.

Low lying wetlands (Haors) and hilly areas need to brought under bountiful sources of agro-production:

According to the Bangladesh Haor and Wetland Development Board, Sunamganj, Habiganj, Sylhet, Moulvibazar, Brahmanbaria, Netrokona and Kishoreganj districts are dotted with as many as 373 Haors. Haors are the wetland areas covered by water almost six or seven months in a year starting from the monsoon. People of haors are to depend on a single crop Boro (variety of rice/paddy) and fishing (only from natural sources) to earn their livelihood. Being the cultivators of a single crop production, people of haor belts contribute a lot to the overall rice production of the country.

As farmers of haor districts are to depend on a single crop of Boro (variety of rice/paddy) to earn their livelihood all the year round, so their sufferings know no bounds because their cultivated crops are damaged totally by the natural disaster (mainly flash flood) that hit almost every year. The disaster not only led to the damage of crops but also deaths of fishes and damaging animal fodder.

Nobody can resist natural disaster to take place. But well organised and comprehensive plan and preparedness may reduce loss of lives and agro-production. Knowing that flash floods may hit the wetlands anytime, the government may allocate sufficient money for sustainable repairing of embankments of haors regards to protecting crops, fishery projects etc.

Floating method or tower system vegetable cultivation might be encouraged during monsoon. Training to farmers and demonstration projects in each upazila by agriculture department/NGOs regarding these methods of vegetable cultivation may attract farmers to implement. Initiatives might be taken to motivate people for cultivating seasonal vegetables & crops in the fertile lands during the winter.

Haor people may be encouraged to opt for commercial fish farming in the sweet water of ponds, canals or rivers. They might be ensured of providing financial and logistic support with training by the fishery department. Livestock department may take initiative to encourage people for duck farming and provide them with training on duck husbandry. Duck farmers might be provided too with logistic & financial support.

The government may take initiatives to grow fruits, vegetables and other hilly environment friendly agro-production beside zoom cultivation providing training to tribal people and monetary & logistic support.

Public and private investors might be inspired to invest in establishing agro based industries in haors and hills. The government might take initiatives to import produced items from these factories.

Ensuring food safety is indispensible:

Because of the recent lockdown due to the disastrous pandemic, the country's overall economy was stalemated and the government's main concern was to feed its poor and poverty stricken citizens. As a significant number of the population is engaged in informal sectors, therefore they were at stake to survive due to losing the means of livelihood.

The pandemic induced mass unemployment and the resulting income loss also worsens purchasing ability on buying foods. Supply side of foods also disrupted regarding production, import and maintain smooth flow of foods to consumers due to lockdown. The country successfully managed the mismatch between demand and supply side of foods during the pandemic by providing poor people with food at free or minimum cost as it had sufficient foods.

During the pandemic Bangladesh was also hit by super cyclone "Amphan" and floods. Natural calamities hit almost every year that cause great havoc on agrarian production. Nevertheless, scarcity of food and uncomfortable price hike of foods was not found anywhere during the aforementioned crisis. Food security saved the government from facing the wails of starving peoples. So, pandemic and natural calamities like disasters have made the need for food security utmost necessary.

Bangladesh should take steps towards increasing agricultural production by utilizing its opportunities like fertile land, irrigation facilities, agro production friendly climate and self-learned agriculture sensitized population. This will ignite heaps of hope towards attaining food security that may lead to restore self-sufficiency in food and to earn foreign exchange by exporting surplus foods.

As agriculture is the only means of food security and also is the livelihood for a significant number of population, therefore agriculture sector needs government direct intervention on issues like launching mechanized harvesting for increasing production, emphasizing on more production of fish, poultry, livestock, fruits etc and ensuring of getting fair price by farmers for their produces.

The major concern of farmers is related to hazard free marketing of their products and getting fair prices. During bumper production and even in lockdown period, they are being forced to sell their products at throwaway prices. It has been seen that farmers dumped hard-earned produce on roads or setting produce ablaze out of frustration as a way of protesting for not getting fair price or not selling their produce.

This is happening because of middlemen's interference in marketing of agrarian products. So, it is the government's foremost responsibility to ensure fair prices for farmers' produce by any means removing middlemen's unlawful interferences in the marketing system. Regarding this, the government may control the primary marketing system.

Like purchase of rice and wheat by the food department, the government may think of purchasing perishable and rotten products with the settled prices. The prices might be determined by the consultation with representatives from farmers and concerned stakeholders involved in marketing. Air-conditioned procurement centers with temporary storage of perishable & rotten agro products might be established in the production intensive areas so that farmers can easily sell their produce at the center with determined prices. Stakeholders such as wholesalers, chain shop owners, exporters etc involved in marketing might be asked to buy products from procurement centers. The whole process of trading at procurement centers must be freed from middlemen's interference.

The Government may take initiative for smooth transportation of purchased agrarian products regarding ensuring safe delivery of products to different destinations. Agrarian products, transportation friendly vehicles and goods trains may operate like launching of Mango/Cattle Train, Postal Service for mango transportation etc. Procurement centers might be administered by the Department of Agricultural Marketing (DAM) and run by the authority under PPP with delegating the power of management.

Chain shop owners or exporters are encouraged to invest directly to farmers by assigning an MOU with DAM on behalf of farmers for ensuring logistic facilities for harvesting, fair prices of produce and other benefits.

Cultivation in Bangladesh is still traditional. It is proven that mechanization in cultivation results in more yields, less money to invest and less time to get yields compared to traditional methods.

Pandemic and natural disasters certainly stressed the new urge to increase agricultural production. So, the country needs to accelerate the process of mechanization in harvesting by ensuring easily available and affordable modern machinery to farmers. Considering the poor economic condition of marginalized farmers, the government may give more subsidies on agrarian machinery and declare a stimulus loan package with minimum interest.

The Government may motivate interested rich persons to establish co-operative fisheries and fish-duck, cattle and dairy farming jointly with farmers in the haors, chars and other swampy lands of the country with ensuring investors of getting complicacy free land, bank loan etc.

Government may build confidence among farmers and make them optimistic to produce more by taking initiatives to establish agrarian products based industries such as vegetables/fish/meat/chicken processing factories, Juice/Jam/Jelly & fast food item factories, factories of milk-made products etc in concerned production intensive areas.

Industrialization in the valued cultivable lands should be stopped by any means. As cultivable lands are decreasing due to river erosion every year, therefore establishment of industries should be encouraged into the fallow and wastelands.

Collaborative efforts might be needed towards achieving desired food security that definitely save people from confronting hunger during the pandemic or natural calamities.

Ensuring of food security:

Ensuring food security for all is one of the major challenges that Bangladesh faces today. Despite significant achievements in production and availability, food security still remains a matter of major concern for Bangladesh. The country has made significant progress in increasing domestic production of food grains. This helped overcome the constraints of national food availability. Yet the acquired food sufficiency is not supportive to fulfill the condition of maintaining sustainable food security. The three pillars of food security as defined by the World Health Organization (WHO) are:

Food availability- relates to the supply of food through domestic production or import, distribution through smooth marketing and exchange.

Food access- refers to the affordability and allocation of food, as well as the preferences of individuals and households and depends on household income, assets, remittances, gifts, borrowing etc.

Food utilization- refers to moth metabolism of food as well as effective use of food within households and communities.

Here are some scenarios regarding production, consumption and utilization of food in Bangladesh.

1. Last few years the country witnessed a bountiful harvest that has been overshadowed by the grief of farmers due to

the low price of crops. Confronting the selling price that is half the cost of production, farmers were compelled to set fire to their paddy field or throw their production to the highway.

2. Big size but costly fishes (Hilsha, Rui, Boal etc), scarce and sea fishes, meat, nutritious food items like butter, ghee, cheese, yogurt etc, essential food like oil except rice, wheat etc are found available in the market but not affordable to millions of people. Despite having the deepest appetite for the aforesaid food items, their income didn't allow them to buy.

3. It was witnessed in the days before lockdown started due to the pandemic, some people bought huge amounts of essential food items, fishes, chickens, meats etc that created artificial food shortages at local markets and eventually encouraged sellers to price hiking. As a result, these sorts of panic create a huge burden to millions of poor people, daily laborers and low-income peoples on their accessibility and affordability to food.

4. Trash bins or waste bins in front of community centers or hotels/restaurants or households usually found a huge amount of wasted or misused costly cooked foods.

The above-mentioned scenarios clearly indicate that food insecurity exists in Bangladesh because of poor food access and utilization of food as overall availability is good and average dietary supply adequacy has been over 100 percent since the 2000s.

Therefore, the indispensable responsibility of the government is to bring inclusiveness in food access as well as proper utilization of food consumption with a view to ensure food security. In addition, the government needs to continue availability of food grains by taking initiatives of increasing domestic production of food grains keeping pace with the increased number of population.

Government may introduce selling of big and scarce costly fishes into pieces or minimum metric units of weight (100g, 200g, 250g) to the retail market as well as all kinds of meats also minimum metric units of weight to make these food items affordable and accessible to all sections of people. Beside, nutritious dairy food items, oil and other essential items, fruits etc may become affordable and accessible to all people keeping the provision of selling these into minimum metric units.

Rationing system might be introduced in regards to selling essential commodities by retailers to remove bad practice of buying huge amounts of commodities during crises or unwanted situations created artificially by spreading rumours.

Making a law of giving fine/penalty must prohibit misuses of foods at households, hotels, community centers, picnic spots etc. Moreover, awareness programs might be broadcasted on social and electronic media to keep people away from misusing food.

The Government should be stressed on continuing bumper production of paddy, wheat, vegetables, sweet water fishes, dairy products, indigenous fruits etc. Regarding these, farmers should be encouraged by ensuring their profession is profitable along with selling their production without facing hazards dispelling intervention of middlemen. Introduction of co-operative farming might be encouraged. Providing subsidies to real farmers for using sophisticated equipment/machines to introduce agro-machineries instead of using primitive methods of cultivation should continue on a large scale.

Farmers need more training and support by agriculture department officials. Marketing system of agro-production should be comfortable and hazard free. Regarding this, an air-conditioned goods train and transport system might be introduced for safe transportation of vegetables, perishable fruits and fishes to different destinations of the country. Chain shop owners may encourage buying food grains directly from farmers with justified market prices. Government may establish agro based industries, air-conditioned warehouses under Public-Private Partnership at places renowned for enormous production of food grains.

Priority to agro-based industrialization:

Bangladesh is a densely populated country. So development of the country mostly depends on active participation of the country's huge labour forces in economic activities in both agriculture and industry. The industrial sector mainly depends on labour intensive garment factories. But it is a touchy sector as its expansion and smooth running mostly depends on GSP facilities, buyer countries' policies, domestic development friendly political environment, economic/business diplomacy of government and intense competition among other neighbouring countries. On the contrary Bangladesh isn't blessed with enough natural resources as raw materials for setting up technology dependent heavy industries. So considering huge manpower with heritable agricultural knowledge and skills the government might utilise them in agro-based economic activities. Labour intensive agro-based industrialisation could be the authentic and rational way of utilising huge labour forces in economic activities that tends to develop growth in the agriculture sector. It also ensures food security in the country with removal of nutritional deficiencies among people. Agro-based industrialisation requires more agricultural products as raw materials and knowledgeable and skilled labour forces as main input. Fortunately the country has fertile lands suitable for over production and skilled labour forces. So, the government should outline more on expediting agro-based industrialisation through encouraging domestic and foreign investors to set up industries using particular agro-based products as raw materials in the areas of the country noted for growing agricultural products abundantly. The government may encourage investors to set up juice/jam/jelly/pulp factories in the areas where mango, litchis, orange, pineapple, jackfruit, watermelon etc grow enormously. Investors could easily invest in producing ready vegetable curry, ready fish curry and ready meat curry. Factories of chips and other crispy & tasty food items from potato, banana, pulses, corn/maize, rice and wheat might be established in the areas noted for growing such agro products abundantly. Investors may be inspired to set up factories of delicious food items from chicken, fish and vegetables like chicken nugget, chicken ball/roll, fish finger/ball/roll, French fry etc. It might be profitable for investors to establish factories of frozen chicken/beef/mutton/fish in packets for cooking. Modern hygienic dry fish factories may be set up in the coastal districts and haor districts (Sunamganj, Natore, Sylhet, Moulvibazar, Netrokona etc) noted for growing and catching fish enormously.

Agro-based industrialisation will create huge demands of agro products as raw materials that will definitely increase agricultural production. Eventually this will ensure food security in the country. On the contrary, excess production after meeting domestic needs may boost exports. Besides this, the country may earn foreign exchange by exporting products from agro-based industries. Moreover, agro-based industrialisation will enable the government to bring a huge number of people under employment. As a result economic activities will actively run in the interior parts of the country that will surely prevent people's exodus from villages to towns only for earning money. This will develop growth in the transportation sector too. Thus growth in the agriculture and agro-based industries sector will be enhanced significantly that will eventually boost the country's overall economy.

Encourage export oriented labour intensive industrialization:

Rapid industrialization is going on all over the country as the government has enabled an investment friendly atmosphere. This trend should be continued by keeping vigilant eye on not wasting valuable cultivable lands. Moreover, expansion of labour intensive and export oriented industries may be encouraged with ensuring utilization of domestic products or resources as raw materials.

Importance of High-Tech and IT based industrialization:

Bangladesh is a relatively young economy. With over 50% of the population younger than 25 years of age, Bangladesh has the advantage of an adequate labor pool that can help drive high-tech (aerospace, pharmaceuticals, computers and office machinery, communication equipment, and medical, precision & optoptical instruments) manufacturing efforts. To cater to the investment needs of the high-tech industry players, the Bangladesh government has formed a dedicated body called the Bangladesh Hi-Tech Parks Authority (BHTPA).

Moreover, the government can accelerate the IT industry and utilise this sector as a platform for sustainable growth. Regarding this, special efforts is needed such as, speeding up IT training/skills; attracting international IT companies/investors (Google, Intel, etc.) to establish IT centres (R&D, Service); and helping Bangladeshi entrepreneurs to start IT companies by providing funds/incubation, sales/business development/marketing support. Moreover, this could also lead to the creation of high income jobs that would encourage foreign trained Bangladeshis to return (thereby reversing the brain-Drain), who can contribute to R&D, and help attract foreign companies to come. The IT industry also uses higher skill, pays better, can be more stable with greater potential for growth than the RMG sector, which is more vulnerable to lower cost regions in Asia and Africa. Development of a more professional sector will encourage youth to seek better education/IT training, generating higher income. Bangladesh can also receive huge remittances from exporting IT labour.

<u>Natural calamities: Initiatives to minimize public sufferings</u>

The nexus between Bangladesh and natural disasters is historically established. It is one of the disaster prone areas in the world because of its geographical location, excessive rivers, land features and monsoon climate. The country has bitter experiences of confronting frequent natural disasters such as cyclones, floods, northwesters, river erosion and storms. But floods, river erosion and cyclones are common disasters that people here face almost every year.

Intensity of cyclones that strike in the last few years the country was so severe but the loss of human and cattle lives were relatively low as a result of timely initiatives taken by the government like construction of embankments and flood shelters, forecasting and warning system, timely evacuation of people and livestock to cyclone shelters, well organised preparedness plans and actions for cyclones etc. But catastrophic cyclones, nor'wester etc. violently destroyed livelihoods of people by wreaking massive havoc on crops, shrimp/fish cultivation, forests and animal husbandry on the one hand and damaging houses, roads, bridges, embankments, infrastructures etc on the other. Post-cyclone sufferings of the affected people know no bounds because of scarcity of food, drinkable water and shelter. Flood and flash flood triggered by incessant rain in monsoon and upper-stream water is a regular disastrous event in Bangladesh that causes serious social and economic losses every year. Flood lasting a long time is a curse to the people. Waterborne diseases break out to add to the miseries of the people. River erosion and tidal surge also have devastating effects causing untold miseries every year. These devour houses, educational and religious institutions, roads, embankments etc.

No government can resist the natural calamities. It rather needs to strengthen management strategies and capacities to minimise havocs, loss of lives, massive damages of crops & agro-production and assets as well as reduce sufferings of people. Measures also need to be taken to enhance people's adaptation capabilities and enable them to quickly engage in income- generating activities staying at home.

During calamities, vulnerable people and cattle badly need to be evacuated quickly to nearby shelter centres from home. Unfortunately, the insufficient number of shelter centres and unusable condition of most of them due to lack of proper maintenance certainly discourage people from going there. A common complaint against coastal people is that they refuse to leave their belongings and cattle behind when the time to move to the shelter comes. Fear of robbery of belongings and cattle, inadequate and unhygienic sanitation arrangements at shelters, absence of privacy for women and young girls, absence of drinking water facilities etc compel them to choose to stay at homes. People with disabilities have no smooth access to the shelters. So, the government may think of renovating or repairing existing shelter centres and construct adequate new shelters with adequate wash rooms, toilets, kitchen room, primary medication corner/room etc. If possible, community clinics might be renovated or reconstructed as clinic cum shelter centres.

There should be the provision of keeping at least one helipad at the top to reach shelters so that relief materials or medication facilities can make easy access to affected people. Moreover, there might be the provision of constructing minimum one 'killas' (elevated mud-built spaces for keeping animals safe) to or nearby the shelters.

The government may encourage well-to-do persons, industrialists and corporate offices to take the responsibility of proper management of these shelters as a commitment to the nation. At the same time, upgrading security measures by law enforcing agencies is essential to keep people's belongings safe and secured. In addition, the government may think of constructing calamity-resistant amphibian houses with uniform design for the poor families of disaster prone areas. Bank loan with minimum interest can be made accessible for economically solvent people to make such types of houses. Trusted agencies might be given the responsibility of constructing the houses for ensuring quality work.

The government may think of providing flats for the climate-change victims like 'Khurushkul Bishesh Asrayan Prakalpa-2' in Cox'sbazar with a view to rehabilitate them as well as ensure their economic solvency. Embankments may be repaired or rebuilt by renowned construction companies having experiences of embankment construction for making these embankments sustainable and endurable to face hazards with optimum level of intensity during calamities. Frequent monitoring is needed for proper maintenance of embankments. Sustainable submerged roads in the cyclone or flood prone areas might be constructed replacing existing roads.

The Sundarbans has once again saved the life of the coastal people from Amphan and Fani as before although its flora and fauna have been damaged a lot. So, forestation with proper care of protecting the Sundarbans should continue. Moreover, people should be motivated to plant water-friendly trees or saplings in the coastal areas so that more than 25% of coastal areas should contain green forest.

The accuracy of the early warning system has also become an issue during cyclones. Inaccuracy in the signaling system discourages people from going to cyclone shelters. So, a modernised signaling system might be launched instead of the traditional system to restore people's confidence in early warning messages by the meteorological department.

<u>Tourism: Could be the best income generating source</u>

Bangladesh is one of the most beautiful countries in the world with an abundance of natural beauties. This is the country with varieties of nature as it has six seasons with different enchanting natural beauties and no other countries in the world have seasonal varieties like Bangladesh.

However, the government and the people of the country are working hard to present the country in the world as the middle income country and already we have achieved a lot of success to make the target achievable. But we could develop more in all indicators of financial performances if we could utilize our natural beauties in a planned way like Malaysia, Thailand and even Maldives. A good number of countries in the world have managed to develop economically utilizing only tourism sectors. Despite having plenty of beautiful and tourism friendly places, varieties of cultures and natures, historical places and cultural heritages, still we are far away from utilizing these to make tourism a profitable industry that could contribute significantly to the economy of the country.

Tourism is one of the fastest growing and single largest industries in the world. The contribution of the tourism industry in the global as well as individual perspective is really amazing. Many countries in the world depend upon tourism as a main source of foreign exchange earnings. This constant growth in tourism throughout the world is encouraging and nations are becoming more concerned about attracting more tourists to their own destinations and trying to promote this sector as a major source for the economic development of the nation. Bangladesh is no exception in this regard. The country is trying from the inception of this industry to attract more tourists to its beautiful destinations and to earn more foreign currency from this sector.

Though the tourism industry and its market have grown phenomenally worldwide, the industry and its market have not grown in Bangladesh. Lack of proper and sufficient promotion is one of the major reasons that stand in the way of the industry in Bangladesh. Potential tourists need to know properly about the attractions, services, facilities, etc. at the destinations and accessibility to there through various forms of promotional measures. Besides, the expansion of tourism business and the increased competition among destination countries throughout the world have necessitated developing appropriate promotional approaches. Due to the existence of intense competition among the destination countries, effective promotional measures are essential for the development of the industry.

Bangladesh Parjatan Corporation or other concerned authorities concerned with tourism in Bangladesh could not meet this requirement due to lack of needed funds along with the absence of decision-makers' foresightedness. As a result, this sector and its market have failed to grow properly because of not reaching the proper messages to the world tourists identifying the country as one of the best tourism destinations in the world. But time has not yet passed. Still there are lots of scopes and opportunities if Bangladesh attempts to highlight it as a tourist destination to the potential tourists properly through an effective promotional measure and can take some initiatives to develop infrastructural facilities towards ensuring smooth access as well as comfortable and safe existence in the tourism destinations.

Bangladesh can offer to the foreign tourists to satisfy their unquenchable needs by the artistic with bounty of tourism resources like natural beauty, sea beaches, forests, lakes, hills, wild lives, archaeological attractions, monuments, handicrafts, sanctuaries, religious festivals, folklore, cultural heritage, way of life, tribal culture etc. We feel proud of having three beautiful sea beaches (Cox's Bazar, Kuakata and Parki) that could easily attract world tourists because of covering miles of golden sands, surfing silvery waves, warm shark free water suitable for bathing, Buddhist Temples and colorful tribal cultures. Cox's Bazar has the longest sea beach in the world and it is called the tourist capital of Bangladesh. Kuakata sea beach is renowned for observing the scenic beauty of both sunrise and sunset from the sea shore making it one of the most attractive tourist spots in the world. The tourists can enjoy the view of the Karnafuli river and the Bay of Bengal together and can observe the big ships anchored at the outer dock, fishermen catching fish in sea, sunset, various colored crabs at the beach etc from Parki beach. We have attractive islands like St. Martin, Moheshkhali, Kutubdia etc which have plenty of natural beauties. St. Martin Island is the only coral island in the country and Moheshkhali Island is famous for hills that could definitely touch world tourists to enjoy.

Bangladesh is a country which is significantly rich in archaeological wealth and major archaeological sites include Mainamoti, Paharpur, Mahasthangarh etc. We have a well known tourist spot named Sundarban. The Sundarbans- the home of world famous Royal Bengal Tiger is the world's largest mangrove forest which is surrounded by beautiful trees (Sundari) and also is crossed by a network of rivers and creeks. There are some other forests like Sal forest in Mymensingh, Gazipur, Comilla region and lush green forests of Sylhet, Mymensingh and Chittagong Hill-tracts have the capabilitiesof attracting tourists from all over the world. The attractive hilly regions in Rangamati, Bandarban, Khagrachari, Netrokona, Sherpur, Sunamgonj and Sylhet have significant differences from the rest of the country because of its indigenous inhabitants (ethnic minorities) who have distinctive colorful lifestyles and cultures that must attract tourists.

We have Kaptai Lake at Rangamati, Foy's Lake in Chittagong, Madhabpur Lake at Moulvibazar etc which are noted for attractive tourist spots. Bangladesh has a big falls at Madhabkunda in Moulvibazar and other small falls at three hill districts that might definitely attract world tourists to enjoy. Bangladesh is rich with the heritage of classical dances, arts and music covering both traditional Bengali artists and the various hill tribes. Bangladesh has also a rich and diverse culture. Bangladeshi culture is influenced by three great religions- Islam, Hinduism and Buddhism. The traditional music, tribal dances, drama and theatre are old traditions and very popular in Bangladesh. Moreover we have kind hearted, generous and laborious people who can easily attract tourists all over the world. The country has also identified some new potential tourism spots like Humhum falls at Kamolgonj upazila under Moulvibazar district, Bichnakandi of Sylhet district and tribals' residences (Punji) in tea gardens in Sylhet, Mymensingh, Netrokona, Sherpur, Moulvibazar etc that may attract tourists a great deal.

Haor could be an excellent destination of tourism. Regarding this, the government may construct flyovers to connect all seven districts within haor with Dhaka by keeping the provision of both road & railway on the flyovers. River cruise might be launched to see the beauty of haor by keeping the arrangement of cultural programme to present Bangladesh to the domestic & foreign tourists. Sightseeing cable cars may attract tourists to enjoy the natural beauty of haor. High rise multi storied towers might be set up in the different parts of haor and there might have cafes of fast foods & coffee as well as internet cafes at the top. Downstairs of towers may be kept open for boat movement and smooth flow of haor water. Arrangements of colourful and well decorated small boats may attract tourists to go to different towers. These towers could also be used by haor people during rain or storm as shelter while transportation. Expansion of tourism in haor districts may create an alternative way of earning source to the local people. Besides haor potential tourism spots should be identified and nourished for attracting tourists so that they have various options to choose haor for tourism

Despite having affluent attractive tourism friendly natural resources, our country is lagging behind in earning a considerable amount of foreign exchanges from the tourism sector. Absence of adequate promotional activities may be identified as the prime hindrance of developing this sector. Inadequate accommodation facilities in the form of establishing hotels, motels, resorts etc with ensuring opportunities for angling, water-skiing, river cruising, hiking, rowing, surfing, yachting, shopping, enjoying cultural show etc in the concerned tourist spots is also responsible for rapid expansion of tourism sector in Bangladesh. Moreover our policymakers have failed to ensure available world class transport facilities to travelers for ensuring smooth access to the tourist spots as well as ensuring proper safety and security in the spots. Besides, no initiative has been taken to beautify tourist spots as well as develop skilled manpower in this sector to provide world class services to the tourists. Therefore GO-NGO collaboration is the only way of removing all the hindrances rapidly to make Bangladesh a suitable, comfortable and safe destination for world tourists. Certainly this will help to earn more foreign exchanges that tend to develop the economy rapidly.

Develop future generation as skilled workforces

There is no denial of the fact that building tomorrow's Bangladesh mostly depends on grooming tomorrow's generation. Proper nourishment of future leaders tends to develop an educated and skilled youth workforce who will be the key to economic development of the country in future for making the government's vision success. Economic development of a country is closely related to increasing rate of economic growth. There is strong evidence that cognitive skills rather than mere academic attainment at educational institutions are linked to long run economic growth. Bangladesh has experienced impressive growth rates in the last few years and the country's growing economy needs educated and skilled people to keep its wheels running.

So, tomorrow's Bangladesh needs educated and skilled workforces. Since the youth workforce is the key to economic development, therefore Bangladesh as a resource-constrained country has to depend significantly on its future leaders as tomorrow's human resources to keep the economic development process moving.

There are many ingredients for the development of future human resources such as education, food, nutrition, health facilities, sanitation etc. Among them education is the most important instrument as it can provide or ensure food, sanitation, nutrition etc. So, education is the first and a foremost weapon of developing tomorrow's leaders with a view to build tomorrow's developed Bangladesh.

But the burning question is- can existing standards and types of education meet the requisite demands for economic development of the country? Education that is provided to children in Bangladesh is categorised into general, technical & vocational (TV) and religion education. But discerning parents and their offspring have more interest in receiving general education because this category of education has huge demands in lucrative and influential administrative job markets.

Scholars argue that countries need a well- diversified education system in order to gain sustainable development through education. The World identified inadequate numbers of educated people in technical education as one of the pivotal causes of Bangladesh lagging behind the desired economic growth.

TheWorld Bank also noted that Bangladesh has no more al ternatives in order to gain development, except properly utilizing its human resources by developing them as educated and skilled simultaneously.

Considering the demand of our economy and the changing global economy, we have to develop a linkage between our education sector and the job market. Currently, our economy is driven by three major sectors- agriculture, remittances and export. These sectors definitely demand an educated and skilled workforce and satisfying the demands, the country will be able to reshape its economy and alleviate poverty. On the other hand, Bangladesh is moving towards industrialization. Indeed, a shortage of technically skilled human resources will be a major impediment to expansion and development of industrialization. Gradually, the country is entering into the era of IT. Business, services, education, office management, banking sector, trade & commerce etc are going to be completely IT based. Therefore, the country crucially needs to develop educated and skilled future generations. As a result of meeting huge demands of a skilled workforce for tomorrow's Bangladesh, the country needs to include vocational courses, Information and Communication Technology (ICT) based education from junior levels to higher secondary.

But the responsibility of not expanding vocationally educated students does not only lie with the government only, parents are equally responsible. Most elite parents and even parents of lower middle class families think that their children should not become a labourer. Even if their children are less academically able, parents try to push their children into higher general education. Social elites and political leaders in Bangladesh also send their children abroad for education. To the contrary, most of the educational policies, access to lucrative & influential job markets and developmental steps are taken for prioritizing 'general education'. So, it is a moral obligation of the government to ensure equal opportunity for students with technical & vocational education (TVE) for their open access in higher education, job market and so on that students in general education has. Moreover, the government may encourage parents to choose TVE for their offspring's education undoubtedly by keeping the provision of appointment of TVE graduates in the top technical posts of the state. There might be a quota for TVE students in case of admission at engineering and technical universities/colleges. Government may take another initiative of opening TVE disciplines in each government school & college although providing good TVE needs more money, internship, management, etc.).

A considerable number of children in Bangladesh have been out of school because of dropout or have never been enrolled in school due to social adversities, unfavourable living conditions because of geographical impediments and last but not the least financial constraints. Work-based learning can provide a strong learning environment and develop job oriented skills to out of school children. Employers must get benefit by recruiting these learners through utilizing productive skills of them. The country also benefited from an increase in skilled labour and ensuring out of school children's smoother transition from school to stable employment without heavy government investment.

Work-based learning is a promising way of engaging never enrolled or dropped out youths to work by making them employable through providing skills development training as well as foundational literacy and numeracy knowledge. Work-based learning provides young people with an alternative way to learn that is a blend of job-oriented and academic. It can provide a bridge into careers, equip them with skills that are in demand in the labour market and connect them to potential employers.

Employers or industry owners' engagement is essential to make work-based learning initiatives for out of school children/youths a success. Therefore, finding ways to make work-based learning more attractive to employers is a key challenge for policy makers. The governments need to motivate employers by clarifying the philosophy of this philanthropic initiative that it not only provides an opportunity for employers to show social responsibility, but also be well aligned with their business objectives. There may be an MOU with the governments and employers for providing logistic and monetary support to run the work-based learning centres as a collaborative initiative. Learners also have a contract with the concerned employers to work for the employers for a stipulated time with the rationale wages.

Work-based learning may promote and develop both academic and skill development, learning of out-of school children and empowering them to become successful in the job market. Their developed job-oriented skills and achieved academic knowledge may be demanded by the international labour market too. Therefore, developing a significant number of out of school children into skilled workforces by nourishing them through launching work-based learning centres should get the most priority to the governments and the following step might be considered by the governments.

The governments may sign an MOU to the employers to run countrywide work-based learning centres providing logistic, technical and monetary support. Curriculum development and management related activities might be administered by the concerned ministry and directorate.

Authorities for exporting manpower may be given responsibility of running skill development centres at district level so that skilled manpower might be developed for international labour market recruitment.

Skill development training courses might be selected considering the learning centre area's labour market demand as well as local natural resources that have alignment to used raw materials by the employers. Target students' family profession may also be considered regarding selection of training courses.

Flexible timetables comfortable to learners may become effective for smooth running of the centres. In addition, the students might be provided nutritious food and a monthly stipend.

Considering massive demand for skilled labour forces in the competitive domestic and international labour market as well as fulfilling SDG targets, the governments may introduce the work-based learning approach for mainstreaming up to the secondary tier of education.

Hopefully tomorrow's Bangladesh definitely will be a more prosperous country if we can build educated and skilled future leaders.

<u>Establishing Good Governance</u>

Development requires performing respective duties with dedication and commitment from not only the politicians, lawmakers and public representatives but also from service providers and policy implementers of the country. Since government officials are the permanent inputs in the development process rather than members of political government, therefore they should have the pivotal role in ensuring development of the country. Development of a country mostly depends on establishment of good governance in public & private offices, policy & law making, implementation of government policies and utilisation of government resources (money, manpower etc).

Good governance is one of the key components of developing a country within the stipulated time set by the political government. Good governance is certainly a combination of sincerity, commitment and corruption-free belief among public representatives, lawmakers and public & private officials. To achieve desired development committed by the political government to the nation, the aim of government administrative machinery should be establishment of good governance. Establishment of good governance crucially demands political commitment through establishing honest democracy and removing all sorts of corruption. Taking establishment of good governance as a vital challenge, the government has taken revolutionary steps in strengthening the activities of the Anti-Corruption Commission (ACC) & the National Board of Revenue (NBR), digitizing the procedures of service providing agencies aiming to keep service receivers' touch away from service providers for addressing the issue of committing corruption. Despite the government's heartfelt efforts of bringing down corruption for establishing good governance, the government can never boldly claim its significant success with regard to addressing the issue. The government may consider the following steps to be taken regarding establishment of good governance:

Elect honest, trustworthy and people's welfare friendly public representatives:

Honesty, trust and candour in politicians are central to the proper functioning of a democracy. Therefore, it is of utmost importance to select the right politicians for running the government as well as contributing significantly as oppositions towards strengthening democracy. As the public see honesty as a core value in our society, therefore selection of politicians with honesty and trustworthiness for running the government alongside with playing a significant role as opposition is inevitable and meaningful. It is most ironic that voters are compelled to elect unsolicited politicians because of the existing system of election. A reason might be that mixes of honest & dishonest and political & non-political people mainly populate the pool of candidates and voters have no choice in this dimension. Making things even more complicated for voters, some candidates typically try to appear honest by mimicking honest candidates' behavior in the election campaign. Moreover, democracy and politics inevitably demands committed and dedicated politicians rather than hybrid politicians.

Consequently, selection of good leaders depends on the quality of the candidates in the electoral race and the information available to voters alongside their development of consciousness in choosing the right person. Therefore, pre-selections of candidates as well as providing civic and voter education to voters can play a major role for bringing effective outcomes in elections.

Pre-selection system of candidates has efficacy in South Asian and African countries where a significant number of voters are economically insolvent, illiterate and politically unconscious to choose right persons as public representatives. In addition, Election Commissions (EC) also need to provide voter and civic education to voters with a view to support voters to bring leaders with honesty and trustworthy within the government and oppositions. The government and ECs may consider the following idea as innovation in election procedure.

There should be the provision of submission of administrative unit wise databases of workers or activists to those who get primary membership of political parties and associate organizations to EC. Political parties need to submit required information and documents of members' to justify their eligibility of becoming party members. This is for online registration of political parties' members and there must be provision of inclusion and exclusion of members with the approval of political parties. A district/province level evaluation committee of EC could be the authority of approving the online registration of parties' members reviewing and authenticating submitted information and documents.

A considerable time before the general election is held, all parties will send constituency-wise possible candidates to the election commission. Listed candidates must have above-mentioned approved online registration of EC. Political parties need to enlist their candidates by addressing equitable issues of ethnic minorities, tribes, religion, genders etc. Candidates for the pre-selection process must have proven honesty, evidence of involvement in philanthropic works, minimum educational qualifications and above all faithfulness to the ideals of liberation war. With a candidates list there must be the provision of submitting information and documents of candidates' source of income, annual income, details of personal and family members' wealth and assets, TIN number and amount of paid income tax, details of any kind of punishment/court case etc. A neutral constituency-wise committee of EC will verify the information and documents of candidates and finalize the party wise preliminary list of candidates. Constituency-wise preliminary list of candidates of each and every political party will be published openly through electronic and print media by EC for getting public opinion about the candidates. After getting public opinion a high-powered central review committee of EC will review and investigate the opinions and finally approve the ultimate list of candidates. Same procedure might be applied for interested persons who may be eager to take part in the election as an independent candidate. Political parties must nominate their candidates from the final approved list for respective constituencies.

In election, voter and civic education are necessary to ensure that all voters understand their rights and responsibilities; political & government system; the contests they are being asked to decide; what type of elections are being held; where, when and how to vote; who the candidates are; values of their verdict; value of democracy and importance of their selection. ECs need to take adequate and effective initiatives to provide voter and civic education to voters. Initiatives such as organization of awareness meetings at villages/slums; broadcast motivational documentaries on Radio, TV, local dish channels and social media; arranging awareness building shows of popular theatre/street drama/folk song etc may take to educate voters.

There should be rigorous terms & conditions as well as code of conduct for candidates regarding expenditure of money, organization of meeting/procession, uses of banners/posters, maintaining peaceful & harmonised atmosphere at election area, respect to other candidates lawful & legitimate rights etc. ECs need to show zero tolerance taking quick punitive action for violating rules & regulations.

Remove corruption:

Moreover, electing honest and trustworthy public representatives, establishment of good governance of a country significantly depends on controlling corruption. Corruption undermines beliefs and moral values in the society and also weakens the whole endeavor of government policy and its implementation. No country can ever claim to remove corruption permanently. Rather each and every country should emphasize controlling the intensity of corruption. Development and excessive corruption can never run simultaneously.

Bangladesh has been doing envious success in every sector of economy and people are observing visible development works nowadays. But they firmly believe that the countries could be developed earlier if diversified and intensified levels of corruption could be controlled. People here mostly are acquainted with fiscal corruption i.e. bribery and embezzlement of money in public and private organizations. But a few people have clear and conspicuous ideas about intellectual corruption that also massively cripples a country's economy.

It is said that intellectual corruption is more detrimental to development than fiscal corruption. It is as heinous an offence as fiscal corruption. Intellectual corruption is ignored a lot as it has no direct linkage to bribery or embezzlement but it is one of the root causes of occurring financial or monetary corruption. It has some dimensions like administrative corruption, policy corruption and political corruption. Although a common type of corruption i.e. fiscal corruption is also seen to occur in aforesaid dimensions of corruptions. The root causes of committing intellectual corruption are nepotism (favoritism), sycophancy, fraud, injustice, blackmail etc.

Administrative corruption is violation of a law for personal benefits by utilization of job position. Administrative corruption is a problem with which the country has been grappling to a larger extent. This erodes people's trust in government and non-government organizations and increases indifference and inefficiency in society as well as hampers development and undermines the rule of law. The consequences of administrative corruption appear in the forms of abusing one's authority position, leaving the client (beneficiaries) dissatisfied, appropriation or abuse of property and assets of the organization, selling secret information of the organization etc. Administrative corruption also occurs in the forms of providing fake or wrong information to policy makers, compelling colleagues to commit unethical or unlawful action, committing unnecessary field visit in the name of organization interest, compelling field level offices to bear all expenses during authority position officials' field visit, buying equipment or stationeries for organizations with excessive price than market price etc. Intellectual corruption goes intelligently but applying dirty tricks, emotional skills, blackmailing, fraudulence and exercise power of authority positions.

Political corruption refers to abuse of power, making false promises and then making a turn around, violating government rules & regulations and instructions of circulars etc. beside nepotism and injustice. On the other hand, policy corruption is a massive threat for economic stability, development and dreadful wastage of a country's scarce resources and money. It is highly detrimental to the advancement of the economy as it increases costs of implementing projects, hampers the growth of competitiveness and brings benefit to other countries or organizations.

Intellectual corruption brings incompetent and unskilled people to the authority positions in policy making. It never ensures the right people to the right positions. It ridiculously ensures reward to bad people and punishment to skilled people as well as increases dissatisfaction and disinterest among dedicated workers to perform duties with commitment and sincerity. It deprives the country to chalk out a friendly and welfare oriented policy that eventually brings a massive loss for the country in the long run. It squanders national resources and reduces the efficiency of government as well as workforces in running policy-implementing machineries smoothly. This erodes people's trust in government and non-government organizations and increases indifference and inefficiency in the society.

So, considering the dreadful aftermath of intellectual corruption the country should stress on controlling it. Fiscal and intellectual corruption are committed by a few numbers of so-called educated people. Illiterate and poorly literate populations are innocent of committing corruption but are the victim of a pinch of corruption in everyday life by a meager number of advantaged corrupted people. So, the country should become stricter to the few numbers of people who commit corruption to bring down corruption to a bearable extent. It is said that the government's hand is so tall that nothing is impossible for the government to materialize its plan.

In addition, good governance too depends on government officials' freedom of working without illegal interference and following government circular strictly. Public representatives should cooperate with government officials to smoothen implementation of government policies without applying illegal interferences. Regarding this all public representatives might supply copies of each and every department's latest circulars and rules & regulations. Public representatives rather monitor and supervise government officials' activities whether they are performing their duties applying honesty and following government circulars or not.

Priority to introduce blended approach of professional and behavioral education:

So, education is the key to ensure development and good governance simultaneously and certainly requires motivated and educated people. But the burning question is - what type of education demands? This is proved that so called educated people are responsible for committing lion parts of corruption or mega corruption. Educated bureaucrats and politicians are the main obstacle towards ensuring good governance. And influential corrupt politicians never want to change the electoral process for giving freedom to voters to choose right country friendly political leaders for honest democracy. So, a traditional knowledge based education system can never ensure development, good governance and honest democracy simultaneously. A comprehensive blended education system comprising Professional Skill-based Education (PSE) and Personal, Social and Moral Education (PSME) could be the most rational and authentic way of achieving countries' overall development by dispelling barriers towards establishing good governance and honest democracy.

PSE is a formalised approach of learning in formal educational institutions through which learners are taught content knowledge and how these are applied in real practice. The learners also acquire the necessary competencies needed for proper practice. Professional Skill-based Education (PSE) is also called career education that involves the skills learners need to be successful in job or career development. Professional education offers many-fold benefits to learners for developing their career path later.

On the other hand, Personal, Social and Moral Education (PSME) refers to helping learners acquire virtues such as honesty, responsibility and respect for others. It helps learners to learn how to live harmoniously in society. It also helps learners to live good lives and at the same time become productive and contributing members of their communities. PSME refers to helping learners to acquire a set of beliefs and a value regarding what is right and wrong. More fundamentally, it encourages learners to reflect on how they should behave and what sort of people they should be. It helps to eliminate problems like violence, dishonesty, jealousy etc from one's life.

Government should come forward to introduce a blended approach of education system to both PSE and PSME at primary and secondary tiers of education for the sake of ensuring overall development and good governance alongside with establishing honest democracy. Out of school children and illiterate young people also need flexible alternative education facilities that must have opportunities of attaining skill-based learning and personal, social and moral learning.

Commitment of telling truth:

Removing corruption cannot happen overnight. So, the country needs to think differently considering it is a time consuming problem to be addressed.

Corruption in Bangladesh has various dimensions and there are many causes behind corruption. This is authentically justified that telling lies definitely fosters corruption. Corruption and telling lies are complementary to each other. Corruption definitely encourages people to tell lies and vice versa - telling lies also assists in committing corruption. People may nourish this bad habit from childhood, never to be changed. So, the country should take steps to resist people from nourishing this immoral habit for the sake of removing corruption.

The government may disseminate a revolutionary idea of telling only the truth amongst people to reduce the extent of corruption. The causes behind committing corruption in Bangladesh certainly have a close link with telling lies. If people of all sections of the community and even the ministers, public representatives, politicians, bureaucrats, public & private service holders, professionals take oath of never telling lies, corruption may come down to a tolerable extent.

The government may start a campaign of "Never tell lies" as a revolutionary initiative. This requires a change in the peoples' attitude and belief. This sort of change inevitably requires change agents and the innocent future generations could be the perfect change agents to make this campaign a success. So, the campaign can be started in all educational institutions of primary, secondary and tertiary tiers of education so that future generations can keep themselves away from telling lies and also the country's future builders can disseminate the message of the campaign to their families, societies etc. On the other hand, family is the best place for nourishing children with the morality of telling the truth before going to educational institutions. Children learn first from the family environment. If they get a congenial atmosphere of telling the truth from family, they will be inspired to tell the truth from their childhood. To encourage children to tell the truth, teachers and family members must never criticize or punish them even when they do wrong.

Development inevitably needs discipline

Malaysia is one of the developed countries in the world that became independent in 1957 with poor economic conditions, no fertile lands conducive to cultivation, shortages of manpower, no seasonal (natural) variation etc. But Malaysia and other South- East Asian countries like Singapore, Indonesia, Thailand and even Vietnam nowadays have been setting inspiring instances to other countries to follow their model of socio-economic and cultural development. The mystery behind impetuous development of aforesaid countries is strong commitment of leadership and establishment of discipline. These south-east Asian countries were not as rich as socio-economic development is concerned immediately after the emergence of independent Bangladesh. But the development scenario of those countries dramatically changed a lot and everybody will be impressed and surprised too seeing the enviable and sustained infrastructural, economic and environmental development along with digitization in every sector. Tremendous development that the countries also enabled to achieve is cleanliness of roads, markets, public places etc and citizens' positive attitude of applying civic senses and etiquettes. The root cause behind the achievement of these countries is establishing discipline in individual and social life as well as all sectors of economy. Thus the pragmatic leader of Singapore, late Lee Kuan Yew rightly said, "I do not believe that democracy necessarily leads to development. I believe that what a country needs to develop is discipline more than democracy. The exuberance of democracy leads to undisciplined and disorderly conditions which are inimical to development."

So, the country's socio-economic and cultural development crucially requires possessing a positive attitude, practices of good manners and morality, obedience of rule of laws and maintaining discipline by citizens. Establishment of discipline relies mostly on carrying rule of laws into effect, the integrity of leadership, good governance and strong will of citizens. The country has a majority of hard working people with the intention of maintaining discipline and obeying rules. This should be utilized to establish discipline with ensuring good governance. Establishing discipline can never be a massive issue to the government as 90-95 per cent people of the country have the tendency of accepting rule of laws. They don't like to commit corruption and immoral activities. They only seek happiness and want to lead life amidst discipline. Only 5-10 per cent of highly educated, influential public and private officials, politicians, businessmen, professionals etc are involved in violating rules as well as committing corruption. Establishing discipline is challenging but not impossible if the government is able to resist the said small percentage of influential persons from committing immoral and undisciplined activities. And citizens believe that the government must be successful as the government is more powerful than others.

Citizens of the country are the only means of putting discipline into practice in everyday activities as discipline has diverse extents to apply in daily life. It includes not only applying civic senses, good manners and morality but also keeping aloof from committing immoral activities. Discipline too has close connection with execution of rule of the laws. The government may consider the following steps to be taken to establish discipline.

Roads/Highways/Waterways, Metropolitan areas, Cities/Towns, Railway Stations/bus and launch terminals/air ports, parks, markets, shopping malls, offices etc might be brought under close watch by installing CC cameras with a view to ensure cleanliness, apply civic senses and avoid creating public nuisance. Culture of giving priority to VIP and CIP's vehicles movement in the highways/roads (except the President, the Prime Minister, Fire Service, Ambulance) must be cancelled.

Highway traffic management and city/town traffic systems must be modernized and digitized. Presence of illegal and unfit vehicles, picking and dropping passengers in the middle of the road, stopping beyond the designated bus stops, removal of shops/markets beside highways, driving by fit and license owned drivers might be ensured. Illegal parking should be resisted. Taking quick exemplary punishment not considering accused status or designation may compel citizens to obey traffic rules.

Rule of laws must be executed by any means. Violation of laws must be brought under rapid punitive action irrespective of social and official status and political identity of the accused.

The Present zero tolerance policy of the government against corruption and unlawful activities should be continued. This citizens' desired policy should be applied not only for politicians but also for public and private officials, businessmen, professionals etc those who are involved in corruption. Agencies concerned to relinquish corruption might be brought under close monitoring too.

Completed development works must have a lifetime and it should be visible to citizens. Moreover, contractors' profit, estimated costs, materials details etc might also be disclosed to citizens.

Commitment in performing duties properly and timely, providing hazardless quality services may ensure discipline in educational institutes, hospitals, agencies of enforcing law & order and other service providing agencies.

Discipline in the tourism sector is significantly important by ensuring tourism-friendly infrastructure, transport, security, amusement facilities, beautification of spots etc so that tourists can choose Bangladesh to tour without any hesitation. Tourism sector could be a vital earning sector of Bangladesh like Malaysia, Thailand, Indonesia and Vietnam.

Last but not the least citizens are to be motivated to obey rule of laws and to apply civic senses in everyday life. Besides, tax payer citizens' honour, priority of receiving hazardless services and patience hearing of problems from government officials must be ensured.

Empowering public representatives to improve civic facilities

People's sufferings due to water logging, flood, traffic congestion, disgusting & time consuming travelling for severely damaged road condition etc are common phenomena nowadays. People are not blaming concern departments or administrative machineries of the country for their sufferings. They blame concerned public representatives although local level public representatives have no absolute power to resolve the crisis to mitigate people's sufferings and ensure peoples' safe, comfortable and hazardless living in society. People only know that they elect public representatives who are the only authority to provide them basic civic facilities and essential services for safe and smooth running of lives in the society. They are not concerned about the policy of the government or of proper authority for addressing the above mentioned challenges for their sound existence in the community. Like other developed countries in the world, people of Bangladesh rationally and authentically demand their elected public representatives provide them desired civic facilities for comfortable living in the society.

This is the beauty of democracy that people will elect their representatives with a view to provide them smooth access to all possible essential services and civic facilities and public representatives are answerable only to the people for their works. Public representatives take power by dint of people's verdict and they are to go to the people's door again after a stipulated time. Evaluating their previous work, commitment and behaviour, people give their verdict. So, public representatives are directly accountable to the people for providing them with best quality services and all sorts of civic facilities.

People of the country expect a lot from their elected public representatives regarding qualitative essential services and civic facilities in return for applying their voting right. It is their firm belief that elected public representatives always stay beside them with their well and woes as well as alleviate people's suffering concerns to receive basic civic facilities like load shedding less electricity, congestion less transportation, quality health service, quality education, quick response immediately after natural calamities hit etc. They have high expectations of enjoying peaceful law and order for safe and sound existence in the community from their public representatives.

People's desired above mentioned demands from their elected representatives definitely require their empowerment and involvement in coordinating all kinds of development works to provide them with essential services and basic civic facilities. To fulfill commitment to voters, public representatives might have legitimate authority over planning, implementing and coordinating all development and service providing issues. Local level public representatives might have a pivotal role in the area of coordination for preparing and designing service oriented plans as well as identifying local resources for implementing plans. Considering local level plans policy level public representatives with the support of concern policy level administrative machineries may develop plans for providing rapid hazardless services to public. Under the directions and supervision of policy level public representatives, all development works and essential services executed by public and private agencies might be brought under coordination of local level public representatives.

People are the owner of the country. So, their desires must be respected and valued by their elected public representatives. Fulfillment of commitments to voters desperately require empowerment in coordinating, supervising and implementing development works or plans for providing rapid best quality services to people. But with the capability of coordination among all service providing agencies and administrative machinery to provide people with quality services, public representatives badly need a skilled, knowledgeable, and committed workforce. And they must be honest, trustworthy, prudent, optimistic and committed to developing them in order to coordinate service providing multi departments' development works.

They need to establish credibility both to public and private officials of service providing public and private agencies. Their role should be impartial and free from nepotism. They should have the quality of encouraging all concerned to abide by government policy by any means. They should not be shown any kind of interest in or persuasion of misusing government money and resources. They might be brought under rapid lawful punitive action with concern departments' officials in case of probing dishonesty, corruption, nepotism and misusing of government funds or resources.

Since public representatives are elected by direct or indirect verdict of people, therefore their thinking and philosophy of work must be confined to provide people with the best quality essential services and civic facilities with a view to ensure congenial atmosphere for people's safe and smooth existence in society. The government may think of empowering them in coordinating and implementing development works and services of field level service providing departments. Local level public representatives' offices might be the centers of coordination of all kinds of development works.

Extent of revenue earnings must be increased

From the very beginning of emerging as an independent country in the world, the government of Bangladesh tried to provide free services to the nation in the health and education sectors. No other country, even a developed one in the world can claim proudly like Bangladesh providing free services in health and education sectors. In recent years the government has also introduced social security network programs of providing allowances to the widows, pregnant women, freedom fighters, old people and disabled people. So, people's aspirations and expectations here in Bangladesh regarding assurances of public services as well as benefits in terms of ensuring social security are high. People from all sections of the society undoubtedly want safe and sound existence in houses and working places, comfortable and safe journey in traveling, available facilities for amusement and recreation, load shedding free continuous electricity facility, adequate facilities of getting gas and water, better quality services from health and education sectors and law enforcing agencies etc. Rendering quality services to the people in the said areas is very much related to government earnings. No government in the world can ever fulfill its people's demands for smooth, comfortable, safe and complicacy free living in society without generating a significant amount of income. With a view to fulfilling people's demands, the government needs to construct and repair roads, flyovers and bridges, establish new power plants for electricity or renovate or repair existing power plants for meeting electricity demand and take initiatives for exploring new gas fields. The government also needs to develop health sector by increasing number of doctors & nurses and supplying latest diagnostic equipments and medicines with other logistic supports in the hospitals and health complexes, develop education sector through increasing trained teachers with facilities for providing quality teaching-learning, construct or establish park or amusement spots and ensure peaceful situation of law and order through appointing rational numbers of law enforcers with adequate modern equipment. To implement these massive development programs the government requires a huge amount of money to spend. The government has two alternatives to enhancing income generation for national uplift. Either the government has to borrow from rich countries and international financial agencies with high interest or has to enhance revenue income utilizing internal resources. The first one is cost effective as it definitely increases debt burden for the people as well as requires meeting irrelevant, irrational and unethically imposed terms and conditions by the lending agencies. So, the government badly depends on local resources for enhancing income to meet huge expenses for implementing massive development activities that tend to ensure better quality services to the people rather than reducing reliance on foreign aid. Tax is the reliable, inclusive and strong source of generating income for the government from internal sources. Income tax, VAT and customs are the three vital sources of collecting revenues from tax. Currently, most of the revenue earnings come from the income tax category, which in the past came from customs. In the near future, when a free trade world will effectively be executed, then Income Tax will be first and

VAT will be in second position in terms of generating income.

Government collects tax for serving the people and people also pay tax from a sense of social responsibility with the feeling of doing something for the country. People firmly believe as well as expect that the government must ensure quality services in the public service providing organizations along with meeting all possible facilities for safe and comfortable existence of living in the society in exchange for paying tax. People of the country are very much positive about contributing to the income generating process of the government with the hope that the government must utilize their contribution for meeting desired requirements of living and maintaining quality standards in a safe and hazard free environment like other developed countries' citizens. Rather than children, students, unemployed persons, beggars and old people, all other people i.e. all eligible people have the ability of contributing for the country with the feeling of doing something for themselves and the nation too. This will also establish their ownership on all public assets, resources and service providing institutions that tend to empower them for ensuring proper utilization and protection of these.

To expand the extent of revenue earnings the government needs to bring all the eligible persons under income tax payment according to their actual annual income and also needs to strengthen the monitoring system for generating revenues from VAT with the help of police and tax department officials. Government may supply electronic cash machines to all shop owners/sellers as well as ensure accountability of buyers and sellers making arrangements of regular checking of taking or giving receipts. Besides ensuring this, the government must dispel corruption from departments of income tax and VAT.

<u>Health & education sectors should get priority</u>

Although the government is spending a huge amount of money every year with a view to provide quality services to the concerned service holders of these two sectors, the outcomes in terms of getting quality services from these sectors are not satisfactory. It is inevitable for a country to ensure quality education as well as to provide better quality medical facilities in the process of economic development. Almost 70 to 80 per cent families of the country entirely depend on getting public sector services in health and education. But they are getting inadequate services from these two sectors despite the government's huge amount of investments in these sectors. Because of the lack of ownership of people in the health and primary education sectors, people are deprived of getting quality services. A few years ago all the people including civil society were fully dependent on getting services from these two public sector institutions. So, everybody concerned with these sectors as service providers could feel their responsibility and liability to the community for their services. Nowadays members of civil society along with the middle class section of the community kept aloof themselves from getting services from these two largest public sector institutions. Inadequate logistic support, absence of positive attitude among doctors, teachers and staff to provide quality service, corruption and lack of commitment concerning these sectors compelled people of civil society and middle-class people not to receive services from these sectors. As a result doctors, teachers and concerned staff in these sectors couldn't feel their liability and accountability to the community people for providing unsatisfactory services. On the other hand, those who are receiving services are not able to establish rights of getting proper services. The service recipients in these public sectors are not also unable to use and maintain all resources properly because of lacking ownership. In the modern competitive world you couldn't deny the existence of private sector involvement in health and education services. Therefore, the government needs to ensure quality services to these sectors to bring all the people of the community to choose primarily of receiving services without any hesitation. It depends on supplying the latest modern equipment and other logistic supports, appointment of trained and well experienced manpower, motivating manpower to become committed and possessing an attitude of feeling accountable and liable to community people for their work. On the other hand, service recipients also need to possess a positive attitude of using and marinating government resources as their own resources as well as to prepare themselves for establishing rights of getting proper services. It becomes possible by creating ownership among community people. Without applying give and take method ownership within stakeholders can't sustain.

Moreover the government needs more money for modernisation and development holistically of these two sectors for proving capability of providing services compared to the private sectors. People can come forward to restore their ownership by contributing both financially and physically for getting proper services from these public sectors. Government may think about introducing a 'Health and Education Benefit' (HEB) card for each and every family in exchange for paying a meagre amount of money according to their abilities. The card is renewable for each year. Those who are service holders may contribute more money to get a HEB card as they receive a certain amount of money as medical allowance from the government or the appointing authority. The industrialists, businessmen and well-to-do persons of the community may contribute a significant amount of money to get and renew HEB cards. Those who earn may be identified to possess a card as the head of the family. Under a card all dependents of the family should give an identity number each. In view of his/her annual earning and expenditure, a token amount of money for receiving and renewing HEB cards may be considered for the poor section of the community. It may not be impossible for the lowest income-earning people to contribute a token amount of money to establish their ownership as we can see that almost all of them are using mobile phones. Those who have no income should provide a HEB card free of cost. It may be mandatory for all the family to possess HEB card and without having HEB card nobody or his/her family members can be entitled to receive medical and education facilities from both public and private service providers. It could be better to have the provision that without a HEB card nobody will get any kind of government facilities and allowances. The fee for having HEB cards should not be treated as tax, rather it may be taken as a donation for getting ownership in the health and education sectors. Government may introduce HEB cards (Health and Education Benefit card) to the families (households) of the country in exchange for contributing or donating a meager amount of money as a token according to their ability of annual earnings. Those who are service-holders may contribute more money to get HEB cards as they receive a certain amount of money as medical and education allowances from the government or the appointing authority.

The system should be completely software based and may authorize the Union Parishad to run the system which has expertise on running ICT based programs at field level. The whole system may interlink nationally so that public and private sector service providers may utilize information on the card. The card is renewable for each year. Introducing HEB card governments may earn a significant amount of money each year and utilize the money only in the health and education sectors with a view to providing highest quality services to the card beneficiaries.